WHEN BODY LANGUAGE GOES BAD

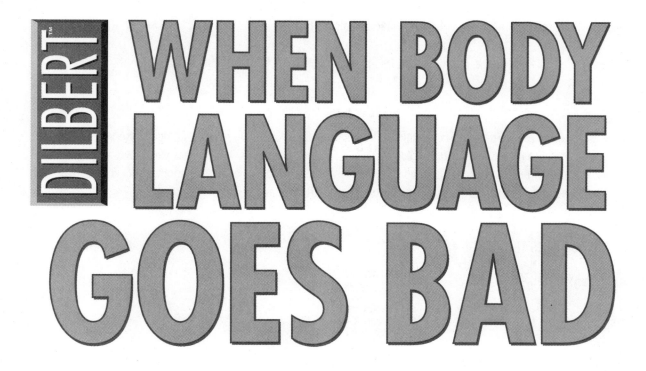

DILBERT™

WHEN BODY LANGUAGE GOES BAD

A DILBERT™ BOOK
BY SCOTT ADAMS

Andrews McMeel
Publishing

Kansas City

——— ATTENTION: SCHOOLS AND BUSINESSES ———

Andrews McMeel books are available at quantity discounts with bulk purchase for educational, business, or sales promotional use. For information, please write to: Special Sales Department, Andrews McMeel Publishing, 4520 Main Street, Kansas City, Missouri 64111.

For Lodi's best product

Introduction

My body speaks several languages and that's not counting the stuff that comes out of my mouth. For example, my knees speak the African clicking language for the first few hours after I wake up. It's a sarcastic sound and I assume they are mocking me. I plan to record it someday and have it translated, as soon as I can find the African clicking embassy.

My face likes to send messages that are wholly independent from my brain. Sometimes my brain will be thinking a happy thought such as "I like cookies" while my face is saying, "I buried a salesman in my basement." This phenomenon worsens when I'm deep in thought. I'll be mentally writing my next hilarious *Dilbert* episode in my head while wandering around at the mall and the next thing I know children are screaming and the townspeople are gathering torches. That, along with the fact that my clothing size is pi, is why I hate shopping.

Needless to say, I am what you might call "unapproachable." I have been going to the same gym for the past ten years and no stranger has ever tried to start a conversation with me. Part of the problem is that when I lift anything heavier than a cotton ball I contort my face as if someone had just driven a railroad spike through my thigh. And on the odd occasion where I initiate conversation—say to ask if a piece of equipment is available—I am handicapped by a severe propensity to mumble. I can overcome the mumbling after I get warmed up, but because I work at home, I often go for hours with no human contact. So my first few words after a silent stretch always come off sounding like a demonic threat.

Me: "Are you done with that piece of equipment?"

What they hear: "I will disembowel you and send your soul to the Dark Region!"

Luckily, both interpretations give me immediate and unlimited use of the equipment. I guess I can't complain.

Another thing I can't complain about is that there's still time to join Dogbert's New Ruling Class (DNRC) and be by his side when he conquers the world and makes everyone else our domestic servants. To be a member all you need to do is sign up for the free *Dilbert Newsletter* that is published approximately whenever I feel like it—about five times a year if you're lucky.

To subscribe or unsubscribe, go to www.dilbert.com. If you have problems with the automated subscription method, write to newsletter@unitedmedia.com.

S. Adams

Scott Adams

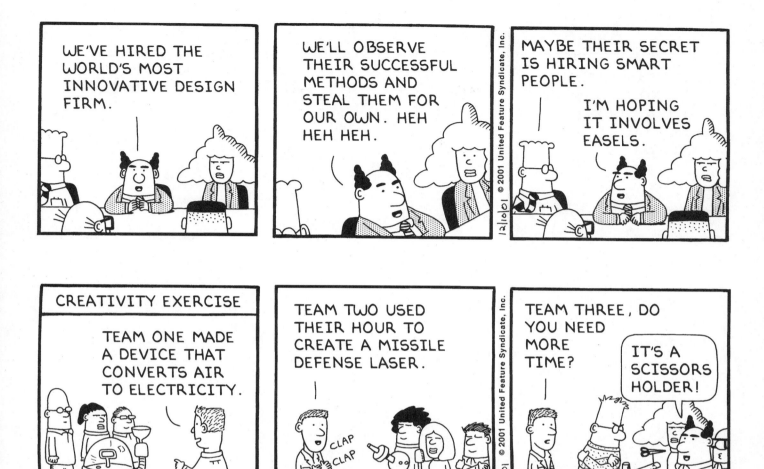

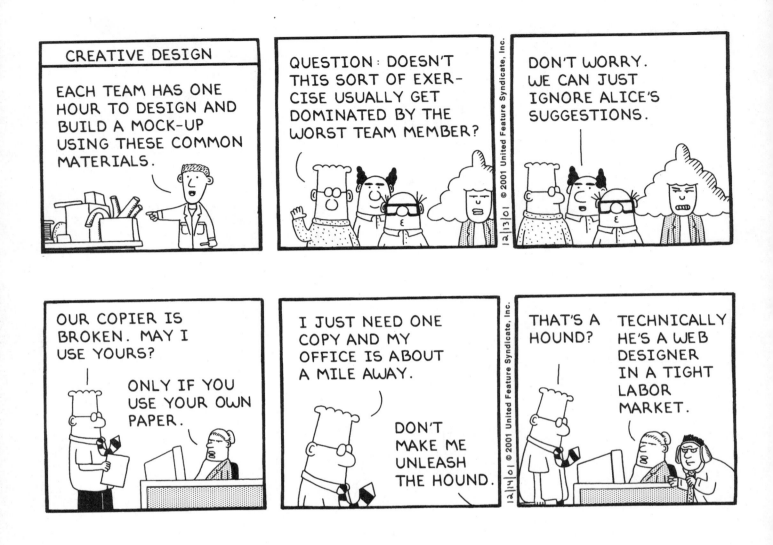

YOUR PROJECT IS CANCELLED. YOU'LL BE DOWNSIZED IN NINETY DAYS.

UNTIL THEN, FEEL FREE TO WANDER AROUND LIKE A ZOMBIE.

I WALK AMONG THEM BUT I AM NOT ONE OF THEM.

HERE ARE SOME PROJECTS TO FINISH BEFORE YOUR LAST DAY.

BUT...I'LL HAVE TO INTERACT WITH PEOPLE WHO KNOW I'VE BEEN DOWN-SIZED.

HEE HEE!

I'LL GET THIS INFORMATION TO YOU RIGHT AWAY. IS NINETY DAYS SOON ENOUGH?

I'M UNEMPLOYED AND I DRIVE AN ELECTRIC CAR.

THESE ARE MY ABS. I TALK TOO MUCH ABOUT MY-SELF AND I'M NOT ROMANTIC.

I REALIZE IT'S A LONG SHOT BUT DOES ANY OF THAT TURN YOU ON?

36

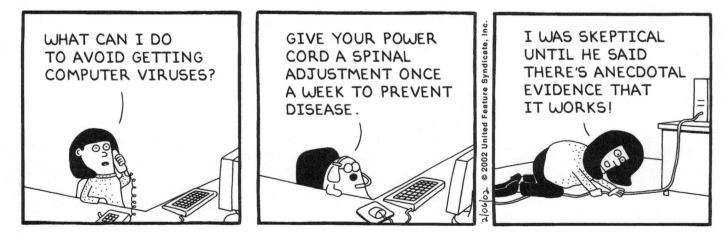

47

I'VE REDUCED OUR DEVELOPMENT COSTS BY OUTSOURCING THE PROJECT.

DOES THE PROPOSAL HAVE A HUGE HOURLY RATE FOR ANY WORK NOT SPECIFIED IN THE CONTRACT?

STAY OUT OF IT.

WHY DO YOU ASK?

WOW! YOU FINISHED THE PROJECT BELOW YOUR ESTIMATE AND ON TIME.

HOLD... HOLD...

ALL I NEED ARE A FEW CHANGES AT YOUR HOURLY FEE, WHICH WAS NEVER SPECIFIED IN OUR CONTRACT.

HOLD...HOLD HOLD.

WAG!

YOUR TRIP IS CANCELED.

WE USED UP THE TRAVEL BUDGET RENAMING OUR CALL CENTERS TO "CONTACT CENTERS."

BUT I NEED THIS TRAINING.

ISN'T THAT ANOTHER WAY OF SAYING YOU'RE IGNORANT?

50

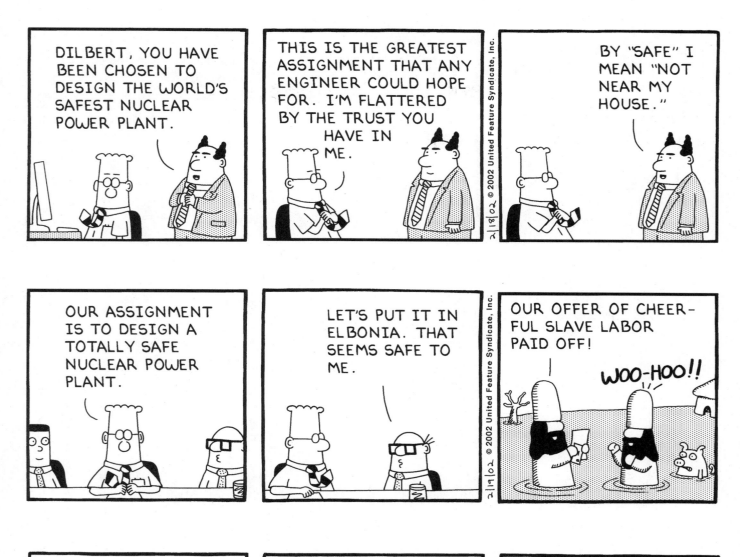

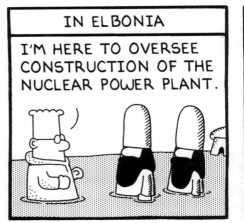

80

89

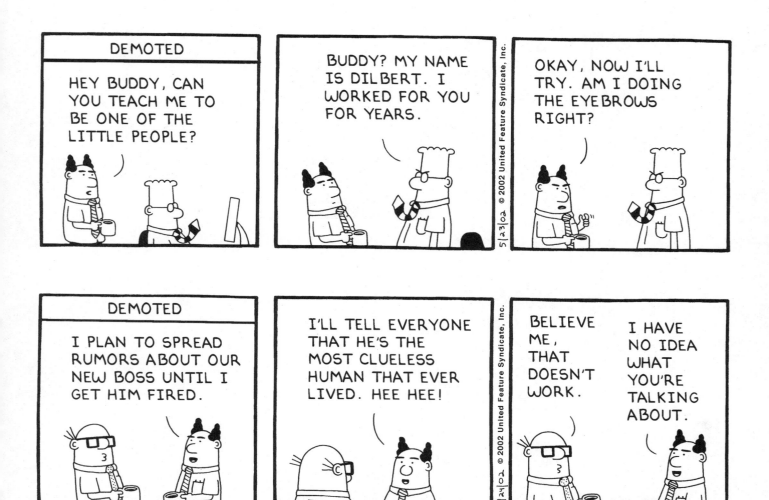

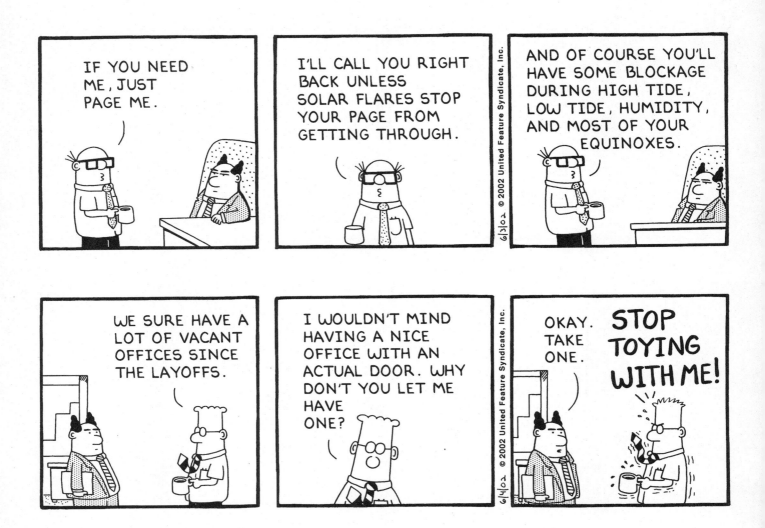

IF YOU NEED ME, JUST PAGE ME.

I'LL CALL YOU RIGHT BACK UNLESS SOLAR FLARES STOP YOUR PAGE FROM GETTING THROUGH.

AND OF COURSE YOU'LL HAVE SOME BLOCKAGE DURING HIGH TIDE, LOW TIDE, HUMIDITY, AND MOST OF YOUR EQUINOXES.

WE SURE HAVE A LOT OF VACANT OFFICES SINCE THE LAYOFFS.

I WOULDN'T MIND HAVING A NICE OFFICE WITH AN ACTUAL DOOR. WHY DON'T YOU LET ME HAVE ONE?

OKAY. TAKE ONE.

STOP TOYING WITH ME!

I'M MOVING INTO A VACANT PRIVATE OFFICE. I GOT THE LAST ONE.

I HOPE THIS DOESN'T CAUSE ILL-WILL IN THE CUBICLE-BOUND CO-WORKERS I'M LEAVING BEHIND.

ALL I ASK IS THAT WHEN YOU ENTER DILTOPIA, YOU BOW IN REVERENCE AND TAKE OFF YOUR SHOES.

OUR ASSIGNMENT IS TO MAKE OUR ACCOUNTING SYSTEM LESS TRANSPARENT.

WHAT?

WE DON'T WANT INVESTORS TO KNOW WHAT WE'RE DOING.

ARE WE BAD PEOPLE?

WE'RE GOOD PEOPLE WHO HAVE BEEN INFLUENCED BY A CORRUPT CORPORATE CULTURE.

OH, OKAY. CARRY ON.

AS REQUESTED, MY PROJECT TEAM HAS ADDED IMPENETRABLE COMPLICATIONS TO OUR ACCOUNTING RECORDS.

AND AN OUTSIDE FIRM IS ERASING ALL MEMORIES FROM SENIOR MANAGEMENT.

HOW DO THEY DO THAT?

OKAY, YOU'RE READY TO TALK TO CONGRESS.

THANK YOU.

I HAD MY CELL PHONE AT ONE EAR AND MY REGULAR PHONE AT THE OTHER.

I'M READING E-MAIL, SENDING INSTANT MESSAGES, MY PAGER IS VIBRATING, AND MY BOSS COMES IN!

YOU KNOW WHAT MAKES YOUR WORK STORIES FASCINATING?

WHAT?

NOTHING.

PROCUREMENT

I NEED TO ORDER A SPECIAL CABLE FOR MY COMPUTER.

NO, THAT'S A PIECE OF ROPE. YES, I KNOW IT'S CHEAPER.

OOH HOO HOO HOO!

WELL, MAYBE IT WAS A MISTAKE TO SIGN AN EXCLUSIVE CONTRACT WITH A ROPE DISTRIBUTOR.

OOH HOO HOO JERK.

MY TECHNOLOGY TEST WAS A HUGE FAILURE BECAUSE I HAD TO USE ROPE AS MY ELECTRONIC CABLE.

OUR PROCUREMENT MANAGER IS A MONKEY WHO SIGNED AN EXCLUSIVE CABLE CONTRACT WITH A ROPE VENDOR.

I'D RATHER NOT TAKE SIDES UNTIL I HEAR THE MONKEY'S VERSION.

I CALL MY IDEA "COFFEE WITH THE BOSS." EACH EMPLOYEE WILL GET ONE HOUR OF QUALITY TIME WITH ME.

I'D RATHER STAPLE A SKUNK TO MY FOREHEAD AND GO TO A TRADE SHOW FOR BANJO MAKERS.

AND YET, IT'S STILL BETTER THAN WORKING, SO COUNT ME IN.

THAT'S THE SPIRIT!

Panel 1:
HOW DO YOU LIKE SITTING IN FOR THE BOSS?

IT'S EASY.

Panel 2:
ALL I DO IS WALK AROUND AND MAKE PEOPLE LOATHE ME WHILE I AVOID MAKING DECISIONS.

Panel 3:
THAT'S ALL YOU EVER DID BEFORE.

APPARENTLY I WAS GROSSLY UNDERPAID.

Panel 4:
MY FIRST ACT AS TEMPORARY BOSS IS REVAMPING OUR PROJECT STATUS COLOR CODES.

Panel 5:
RED, YELLOW AND GREEN WILL BE REPLACED BY WHITE, OFF-WHITE AND EGGSHELL.

Panel 6:
I HAVE TO CONFESS, IT WAS EMBARRASSING TO REALIZE I ONLY HAVE ONE IDEA.

Panel 7:
I'M REFRESHED FROM MY VACATION.

Panel 8:
I AM CALM AND RELAXED.

WALLY SAT IN YOUR CHAIR.

Panel 9:
WE'LL HAVE TO BURN YOUR CLOTHES TOO.

COOTY SQUAD

7/11/02 © 2002 United Feature Syndicate, Inc.
7/12/02 © 2002 United Feature Syndicate, Inc.
7/13/02 © 2002 United Feature Syndicate, Inc.

125

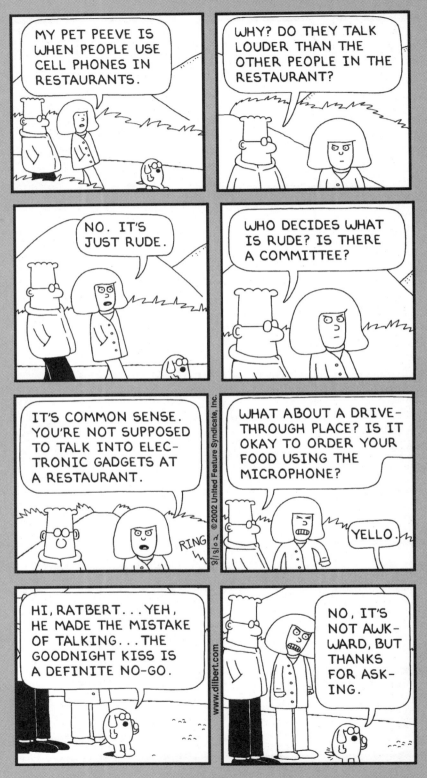